How to use this book

The *Fun With Time* eyePad is a great way for your child to practice telling the time while developing their vocabulary. With adult guidance, and using the photographs as talking points, your child can relate to the connection between the clock hands and times of day.

This eyePad can help your child to understand many different aspects of telling the time, from reading the hands on an analog clock to learning about the days of the week and the months and seasons of the year.

The first section of the book encourages your child to draw hands on clock faces and to pay attention to the correct position and what time the clocks are showing. Be sure to praise your child for effort when they get something right.

The next section is all about understanding what the time is, and asks your child to fill in the blanks. The "odd one out" and "match the time to the clock" puzzles help children to practice their knowledge of time-telling with ease.

The rest of the book helps your child to practice thinking about their daily routine and matching timed events to the clocks, while introducing the seasons and days of the week.

When it comes to writing words, such as days of the week, tilt the page left or right slightly, depending on which hand the pen is in. Right-handed children benefit from a page tilted to the left and left-handed children benefit from a page tilted to the right. Use the numbered arrows to help your child trace then write the words.

Learning is fun. Try to make up stories about the pictures on the page so your child relates to them while learning.

At the end of the book there's a word search, so be sure to help your child identify the words they've come across while using this book.

Remember to reward with a gold star for good work!

The long hand shows the minutes.

The little hand shows the hours.

Trace the hands on the clock face.

It's 3 o'clock.

Trace the hands on the clock face.

It's 8 o'clock.

Where is the little hand pointing?

☐ o'clock

Where is the little hand pointing?

☐ o'clock

Where is the little hand pointing?

☐ o'clock

Which clock is the odd one out?

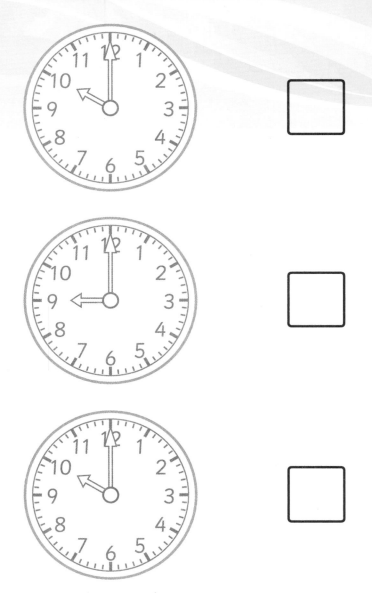

Which clock is the odd one out?

Match each clock to the right time.

2 o'clock

8 o'clock

7 o'clock

Match each clock to the right time.

3 o'clock

6 o'clock

1 o'clock

Draw in the little hand to show the right time.

 3 o'clock

 5 o'clock

 7 o'clock

Draw in the little hand to show the right time.

 4 o'clock

 1 o'clock

 10 o'clock

What time do you wake up?

Draw in both hands.

What time do you have breakfast?

Draw in both hands.

What time do you go to school?

Draw in both hands.

What time do you go to bed?

Draw in both hands.

What time do you eat lunch?

Draw in
both hands.

What time is night time?

Draw in
both hands.

What time do you play?

Draw in both hands.

Draw in both hands to show the right time.

7 o'clock

2 o'clock

What time is lunch time?

Draw in
both hands.

Draw in both hands to show the right time.

5 o'clock

3 o'clock

What time do you have a bath?

Draw in both hands.

Draw in both hands to show the right time.

1 o'clock

10 o'clock

When would you see an owl?

☐ Day

☐ Night

When would you see the moon?

☐ Day

☐ Night

When would you see the Sun?

☐ Day

☐ Night

When would you see a rainbow?

☐ Day

☐ Night

There are 12 months in a year. Trace each name.

January

February

March

April May

June July

August
September
October
November
December

Which month is missing?

March

January

April

June

November

October

May

August

December

February

September

Which month is missing?

August

December

July

September

April

June

March

November

February

January

May

Which month is your birthday in?

. . . .

Which month is Christmas in?

There are 7 days in a week. Trace each name.

Monday

Tuesday

Wednesday

Thursday

Friday

Saturday

Sunday

Which day is missing?

Sunday

Thursday

Tuesday

Monday

Saturday

Friday

Which day is missing?

Wednesday

Sunday

Tuesday

Monday

Friday

Thursday

There are 4 seasons in a year. Trace the name of each season.

Spring

Trace the name
of the season.

Summer

Trace the name
of the season.

Autumn

Trace the name of the season.

Winter

Which season is this?

Spring? Summer? Autumn? Winter?

....

Which season is this?

Spring? Summer? Autumn? Winter?

....

Which season is this?

Spring? Summer? Autumn? Winter?

· ·

Which season is this?

Spring? Summer? Autumn? Winter?

Time word search

Find the 10 words from this list:

season   autumn   minute
clock   day   hour   week
month   year   night

a	w	r	y	s	e	o	p	f	s
l	b	i	y	e	a	r	l	n	z
d	k	u	n	a	l	z	b	v	o
m	a	o	h	s	e	r	s	x	m
b	i	y	m	o	n	t	h	c	u
d	h	n	v	n	u	w	p	l	b
a	u	t	u	m	n	r	b	o	e
y	v	l	e	t	i	j	a	c	l
c	q	d	b	w	e	e	k	k	h
b	m	r	y	e	n	i	g	h	t